Books by John E. Roessler

Thirty Pieces of Silver

Your Heart My Renaissance

Poetry for the Modern Age

Was it the books read, TVs unpurchased,

years unlived, dreams created

on thoughts recently shared?

Eucharist shared, mass lived,

Ben and Jerry's, Leonard Cohen, Rilke,

Whitman, City Lights, Kerouac?

Was it when I read to you,

when you played for me,

when time stood still for you to hold?

ACKNOWLEDGMENTS

For the innocent, who believe good triumphs over evil.

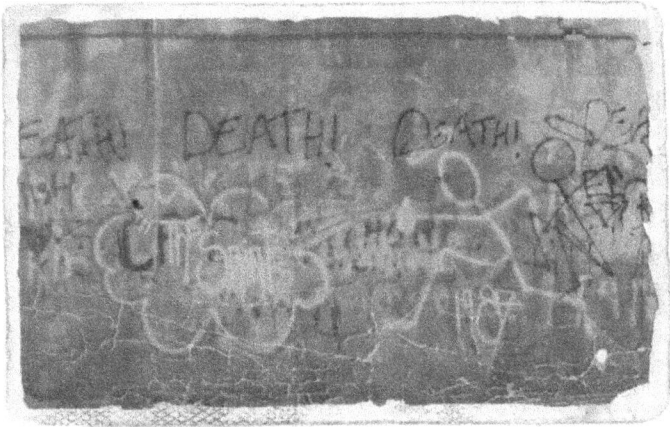

DEDICATION

Dreamers and wanderers unite on the path of love, life, and spirit …

Thirty Pieces of Silver

Thirty Pieces of Silver

Poetry and Words by

John E. Roessler

CONTENTS

Love

Life

Spirit

Words ~~~

Chapter One

Love

My Love Cannot Change

My love for you cannot change,

I won't let it.

It's tried – fiercely, stubbornly;

tried to grow both ways,

apart like a splintered Oak

and at other times closer –

to a space where I lose myself.

I won't let that happen.

I am too comfortable here.

And there tends to be safety in comfort –

a familiarity.

Like when you smile at me

and turn your head just so – quizzically,

wondering.

Too close or too far

and I'd miss these nuanced moments –

losing myself in you or turning away

seem equally unacceptable,

for you would no longer see a smile

reflected within my eyes.

Where Did It All Begin

Where did it all begin,

at the river, in the kitchen,

over a bowl of roasted garlic?

Was it the poetry Jack gave you,

enhancing your romanticism?

Was it at Pier 39 when your sugar dropped

and you held on to grace,

waiting for your clam chowder and sourdough?

Or even earlier, the touch by the water,

fall bonfire, smoke-burned eyes

on Oregon's windswept beaches?

Camping with herons,

lightning storms or hawk feathers?

Was it the wedding at the Saturday Market,

the Beetles' lyrics we shared,

my sum total of three guitar chords

and our love for U2?

Was it the sweet grass, the futon,

spoken truth shared

(the knowledge that distance can be safe)?

Was it the red, burning moon, the Loa Temple,

our refusal to roll over and die,

the tears you kissed from my face – falling?

Pendereski's triumph over Eugene?

Was it Smoke Signals,

stories told, music played, hearts opened,

lyrics written, kisses accepted, time wasted?

Was it your prayers, my desire,

your understanding, my fear?

How did you know I cared so,

when I swallowed my soul

and told you about all of me?

Was it the books read, TVs unpurchased,

years unlived, dreams created

on thoughts recently shared?

Eucharist shared, mass lived,

Ben and Jerry's, Leonard Cohen, Rilke,

Whitman, City Lights, Kerouac?

Was it when I read to you,

when you played for me,

when time stood still for you to hold?

You knew all along that I would wait for you,

that I will come to you.

I die slowly within our cyclic separation

and live a thousand lives each moment

I breath your essence (from within your body).

We have lived a lifetime within this moon's
journey.

Eucalyptus and the root of an unnamed child

stretch toward a candle you hold.

Woodgrain and Burnished Metal

Woodgrain and burnished metal

construct my world.

One of smoke and dusty floorboards.

Where I walk leaves a trail,

sometimes leading nowhere, for nothing –

sometimes.

Is there meaning in the moments –

in the finger touches,

in-between breath and hunger?

Here the haze breeds wonder gently,

like a lover's falling heart.

Guinevere

I feel like I know you.

Have we met before today,

when youth was confusing,

a nervous gesture?

Or maybe it was another life,

when you were Guinevere,

in the lake of my tears

summoning motionless?

You are as beautiful as you always were,

virgin eyes and creamed skin,

your parting lips pronounced my name

like a foreign language;

please tell me more ….

The Contagion

When the contagion is a smile

and the neurons jump

then why do you desire to flee?

Is it authenticity – is your filter working?

Or do you live in opposing hemispheres

where right is left, good is bad,

and trust has been eradicated?

I can barely see you at that distance.

Will you run to the right now so I know it is you?

Each Drop of Water

Each drop of water

a prism of burning flesh

as ice became no more.

Racing south

to form the river of your body

where love, borne of life's longings,

never reaches the ground.

I watched as the river widened – entranced.

My fate to be washed by eternal waters,

warmed by the beating heart,

colored by pure white flesh.

A fragrant wild rose

draws the blood that loves it

as we pen our destiny in this red ink.

The Hawk's quill flies

from river bank to river bank;

your sweetened breath gives rise to urgency;

our rivers become one.

The sea is love.

The Burg Calls

The Burg calls like an alpine melody –

pleasantly echoing.

This rustling forest as uneasy as my heart.

No bird's song and dance brings peace.

Time has passed, yet sun-up, sundown,

and all moments in-between

hold but one thought – you.

Much help comes

in the form of advice and introductions.

These meanderings the panacea,

yet fail to hold my attention.

You've left nothing untouched in my world.

I take you with me, for you live within.

Again, I realize the depth which you've reached.

I do not understand the disposable nature of love.

How, when words fail and eyes speak

these notions are not eternal.

How is it that we accept less

in matters of the heart?

I cannot deny my ignorance of love;

my struggles when evil disguises itself so.

Over time love has shown her face to me.

There comes but one.

Is this Dante's purgatory – her absence?

The Hawk will not enter

and my friend the blackbird

has left me in the dead of night.

No need for song – dead men can't dance.

The time has passed

when love felt my every thought.

Herbs, oils, and potions of love

do not find their way here.

The dove beyond, sits with its soulmate.

My hope is it's not forsaken on its journey.

Do not watch me closely my little dove

it will change your life.

For when the dead speak

those who cannot hear, listen.

They gather, shy of the living,

waiting, forever waiting for the coo,

feathers held close, for flight is but a dream.

The storm comes now, it is right on time.

I am the thrush the farmer has left behind.

To go with the wind's desire,

always longing, whenever home.

I am the discarded seed

laying in next year's compost.

Love will not return here.

Others must bury your dead.

The Pacific and I

There is something odd about our union,

the way I come to the shore

and never furthermore – these days.

We have known each other for a fair time.

I raised my children by the ground squirrel

and tide pool.

Played with foreign languages here,

the lion's bark notwithstanding.

This is Lover's Point

and I suppose it was for me once.

Now it is but memory's tide,

loosened upon me like the soft air – it is cold here.

The sun leaves our grasp

at this exact point of earth.

And soulmates dance on the rocks,

a mating ritual.

Is it fair for me to watch on – longing?

Good Morning My Fair Lady

Good morning my fair lady

lay here while I make you tea

I felt you toss and turn last night

you were restless up against me

Was it your dreams that caused distress

Or was it this life more or less

Let me brush the hair

back from your face

Let me wipe the sleep from your eyes

Let me commit to our destiny

a mutual heaven in a common sky

Good morning my lady

none of these emotions we feel

run in black and white

They explode at our union

into water-colored light

You bask in this early morning

wrinkle of linen

I am breathless as I absorb

your beauty in

Let me draw for you a bath my love

Let me brush your intense hair

allow the cream to soften

your moment

Let my hands speak their care

I am your morning sonnet

I am your dream

You taste me on your lips

You slide from what's real

I was borne for this moment

from the ocean to the stream

One of God's many gifts

shades of color within the dream

Let me dress you in white my love

a crown of daisies from your prince

Let me adorn you in delicate lace

allow a touch of herbal essence

Lady I honor you

your single breath

Lady I devour your moment

I savor your soul

for you are peace and your calm leads our hearts

Pretending

Sometimes I have to pretend with you,

and then you pretend not to notice me pretending.

It can be confusing,

not really knowing

if it is you that is pretending – or I.

Or even worse – neither of us.

Chapter Two

Life

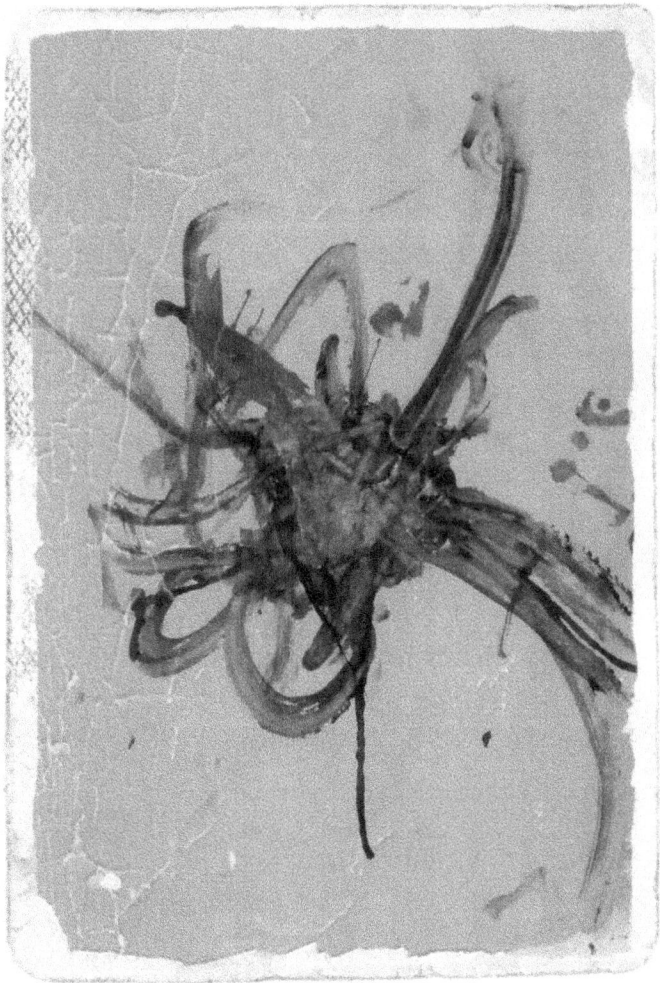

Color of Darkness

Sound defines night perpetual,

while a wisp of grey decreases

our hoped-for permanence.

Whisper – it helps push back the night.

Teetering on the soft edge

an unintentional foothold sought.

Black noise and water drops reach you.

[There is] a settling of mind and purpose.

Knowledge becomes your candle,

flickering, growing brighter.

The whisper – your lips surround.

Did you say, "freedom?"

Distant Shores

Steadfast wind pushes the banks around me –

protecting.

As the sun climbs and draws

its singular line directed at my new day.

The constant roll of ocean wave

an effervescent white noise

purifying the ailments, we carry here.

These human worries

of money, health, and longevity,

nag at daily existence,

crying to the shore to be set free.

We are surrounded by crabs,

walking sideways, burrowing against the

impending heat.

I can't count them all – each with its life-lesson.

They are working hard to clear the place,

cleaning and building.

Only to be pressed upon by the heavy footed

beach-goers looking for solace.

~

August has come and I long for a spring do over.

Love is in the air.

Destiny and Fortune

Destiny and fortune war

over this consummate soul.

A warrior's plate and name,

red and cracked through

for a spurious honor.

Is it God or Country, oil or water, we covet

at the threshold of sanity?

This barren path of ignorance,

crag and pit prevail.

The return is lost in darkness.

Fate is a double-edged sword

sharpened by time and distance

from the Carpenter's stone.

This petrified forest planted by the Gods

is silent like death.

Nature has closed her eyes in horror –

cold sets in at the bone,

and fortune gathers her wares.

The lament is echoed through the child's heart.

Echoed through the child's mind.

Echoed through the child's innocence.

Echoed through the child.

Touché your poetry tears the soul,

resilient but not invulnerable.

The seeds of the hero's death

are carried on a black wing,

sown by law and nurtured

in the heart of his free will.

Call to arms your forces

and march into *Odyssey*.

You command a spiritless force

within the mind's eye

and pay the toll of castrated dreams.

Jesus was not the last one to call to His Father.

Orchid

The orchid breathes

from a celestial wood,

a dynasty; a constitution.

From fire to water –

birth and tradition unite a people.

Perpetual smiles.

Teeth

The teeth in my zipper

have more of a bite.

The spiral in my notebook

does more work.

If I was to count these cars – endless.

They roll by as if there is a destination

more Grand than the present.

Drivers with fingers stuck in noses,

stuck in the air;

playing bumper cars with cell phone ears

wagging.

Family Affair

T'was a family affair.

One in which too much is consumed,

food, rhetoric, and one another.

Small talk, big talk, and shared jealousies,

none quite too obvious.

A prodigal son, a proud father.

A fatted hog and horn of plenty.

Where is she going, her hair and her dress

matching the hues of a more promising world?

This wavy bowl blown to perpetually smile,

grimace, then smile again.

A life-tape in playback.

Denny's Route 30

Another diesel diner

at a crossroads in Amish town.

Shuster's name displayed

on the mounted dinner plate

while the overweight waitress

tells you what you want.

It takes three tries to get a waffle and an egg.

There are no mustaches on the men – save me.

And the beards speak of status

as they point towards their over easy eggs,

jiggling with speeches of barn-building and

needed rain.

My waffle is stamped with the café's name

and I notice how tired I am.

I notice I have yet to begin.

I'm a back against the wall kind of guy.

I look for a magic marker to sign the plate.

Crime of the Century

An occupied Maryland looked South,

beyond the Potomac.

Gentlemen farmers,

secret agents,

three of prominence

under the bullet and the blade.

"Sic semper tyrannis,"

a Nation mourned undivided in '65.

Paper Walls

If I take this task given

as less serious,

is it less in its seriousness

to you who has so graciously

found me wanting?

And who then am I

to find my nose raised

at tea of Bergamot

or boot of leather?

Is the time spent here

within these paper walls

considered a productive

form of ass-whipping?

Am I receiving sustenance

or is the task its own reward?

Metro Musing

Metro life is beyond culture – a sub-way culture

to be more exact.

The roll and lull of the dilapidating cars.

In and out of tunnels, above and below grounds –

National unaffiliated grounds.

A microcosm of our genus: living, loving, longing

– anger coexisting with the joy of travel.

We ride because of convenience.

We die because of convenience – not all by choice.

Death sneaks onboard,

jumping the turnstile,

lifting the track,

fraying the wires,

and pushing the willing

in front of approaching steel.

None volunteering to witness – heads down,

eyes turned as if poverty has called,

its outstretched hands quivering

while electronic bells chime:

"Step back to allow the doors to close."

Chapter Three

Spirit

The Ritual

I closed my eyes and said a prayer,

turned fully around three times

and opened them –

knowing that you would not be present.

Yet, the ritual brought me a momentary

sense of peace.

Soul Desires Spirit

Soul desires spirit's inward journey.

You awaken my darkness.

It steps forward into the light.

You cannot look on as

brilliant wings unfold.

I fly to you.

Black and White

I found myself followed this day

by my mysteriously blackened bird.

Shades of blue flashed at me

from parted wings in extended flight.

A slow, even, movement

beckoned my attention

allowing me to live within its presence.

I've lived this day before.

Some may label these darker feelings depression,

the manic call from this bird named Sabbath.

Others, a needed journey to the blackened depth

of the wellspring of life.

It's among Rilke and Neruda

I sit at tea hour

waiting for the turning of pages

to move me from night to day.

The teas were sweeter yesterday,

the hour longer,

the crucifix taller,

the spirit-flame burned brighter.

This white candle sealed in chrism is wickless.

My poetic friends say much

as the sea's foam turns

from white to black in solitude.

I don't recall this heart's intense beating

or lungs which will not reach their capacity

existing before today.

The tea is bitter

and no fruit may be had for sweetening.

Is this Pentecost,

the day you choose to pay me a visit?

Should I set a perch for you near my door?

The river runs cold this time of year

and there is no certainty

waiting in the mists of your heart.

Your night cannot see beyond the

vision of its own soul.

Please let me rest now my friend.

Your incessant calling

provides no comfort in this ebony hour.

Your blue-black eyes bring my only chill

as my soul escapes me.

Wingless

Stay away from my love.

I'll pluck your Angel wings and

spread the feathers to the four winds.

I'll stifle all your screams

and it ain't even worth it,

the price you must pay to

fall from such a height –

it ain't right.

You were wounded in the birth canal.

You were wounded on the street.

You've damaged a soul

but you don't know how

as you turn from those you meet.

You tell us what you need,

then you start to bleed.

You show us what you fear,

then you draw us near.

You pass yourself on the crosswalk

and never even glance.

One running from fear

the other from romance.

You want to take the hand.

You want to burn the cross.

Your robe is torn and frayed.

Your words are forever lost

(or so you say).

Poor Man's Faith

I went to the father

the other day.

Asked him to sit awhile and pray.

He said, "I am sorry son,

you are on your own

with these decisions

that you've made."

Then the Church exorcised my girlfriend,

took her to a higher place.

Now I am alone with my poor man's,

my poor man's faith.

Other night in a dream it came to me.

I lost my entire family.

I turn to her and she was not there,

all I got was the wall's blank stare.

Then I was standing at the pearly gate.

St. Peter's eyes told "It's too late."

Now I am alone with my poor man's faith.

Check my mail most every day,

just to see if she's thinking my way,

Is she alive or did she pass away?

For now, I am alone with my poor man's faith.

Restless

The towers are down – it is final.

It could have been me – it is finished.

I was guided to St. John,

he with his locusts and wild honey.

It is a ceaseless calling to end the hatred within;

like the New York skyline ever-changing.

And I the martyr with the rope and the sack cloth.

The past beckons me sweetly at night –

it is all that I have.

The annulment has proceeded like the death of a

soul – unstoppable.

Burl wood and ivy-terraced kingdoms hold a

respite for the little boy inside.

Yet, I suffer.

It is the loss and the unrepairable flesh.

The weight of my world has become an

unbearable lesson on an unpaintable wall

I have failed to cleanse.

The road calls the restless and I obey.

The Light

I was asked to cultivate the light inside,

to bring it from outside and fill this empty

cavernous body.

I was asked to run to myself and sit,

watching as my reality passed by –

breathe and transcend.

When the body is no longer a concern,

when the space between thoughts

is all that remains,

when time and light touch,

true meaning becomes constant.

The Buddha and His Teachings

Excessively delicate

But not discouraged

[a] compass of loving kindness

Futile self-mortification

By example and by precept

Endeavored to enlighten

Spirit of free inquiry

Discourse of birth and death

One pointedness of the mind

The pleasant and the unpleasant.

The End

The end is always near,

at least the end of something,

as is its beginning, another will follow.

We've been shown this way,

this circular path of breathe

and gasp, slap, and scream.

Reinventing our own survival

we awaken again and again.

I will hold the cup while your soul nourishes.

Fly love, fly,

and let the wind blow you into my arms.

Spirit Guides

Maybe with some concentration

at thirty-five thousand feet

I can be closer to God.

Suspended here, floating,

compressed in an unnatural air,

a human condition,

racing with the spirits.

"You there, can you point the way to Chicago,

the city on the lake,

where Orthodox cemeteries hold the dead;

youthful photos on display

locking them in time – their time?"

A window into what lies below

I wonder, have they met God?

Is this where I should be looking,

walking among our ancestors,

in unmarked pauper graves?

I know she is here,

debating with the spirits,

testing their patience,

going through them one-by-one,

looking for the final moment.

Maybe someday she will introduce me

and we'll take photos together.

End Matter

A few facts of interest:

1. My Love Cannot Change – written on August 21, 2016 in Alexandria, Virginia.

2. Where Did It All Begin? – written on October 12, 1998 in Sierra Vista, Arizona.

3. Woodgrain and Burnished Metal – written on August 22, 2015 in Alexandria, Virginia.

4. Guinevere – written on September 1, 2016 in Alexandria, Virginia.

5. The Contagion – written on September 10, 2014 in Alexandria, Virginia.

6. Each Drop of Water – written on June 26, 1999 in Wiesbaden, Germany.

7. The Burg Calls – written on July 1, 2001 in Freiburg Germany, Kreis Augsburg.

8. The Pacific and I – written on September 6, 2001 in Monterey, California.

9. Good Morning My Fair Lady – written on May 24, 1999 in Route 32, Maryland and finished on June 6, 1999 in Altoona, Pennsylvania.

10. Pretending – written on August 21, 2016 in Alexandria, Virginia.

11. Color of Darkness – written on May 31, 2010 in USA.

12. Distant Shores – written on August, 2015 in Outer Banks North Carolina.

13. Destiny and Fortune – written on January 21, 2001 in Sofia, Bulgaria.

14. Orchid – written on December 1, 2012 in Alexandria, Virginia.

15. Teeth – written on March, 2004 in Crystal City, Virginia.

16. Family Affair – written on November, 2012 in Alexandria, Virginia.

17. Denny's Route 30 – written on March 20, 2002 in Breezewood, Pennsylvania.

18. Crime of the Century – written on May, 2015 in Alexandria, Virginia.

19. Paper Walls – written on March, 2004 in Crystal City, Virginia.

20. Metro Musings – written on July 21, 2016 in NOMA to Huntington, DC Metro.

21. The Ritual – written on August 15, 1998 in Laurel, Maryland.

22. Soul Desires Spirit – written on January 31, 1999 in Guilford, Maryland.

23. Black and White – written on June 23, 1999 in Borders Café, Columbia, Maryland.

24. Wingless – written on August 8, 1999 in Dexheim, Germany.

25. Poor Man's Faith – (lyrics) written on June 15, 2001 in Worrstadt, Rhineland, Germany.

26. Restless – written on October 8, 2001 in Monterey, California.

27. The Light – written on September 6, 2014 in Alexandria, Virginia.

28. The Buddha and His Teachings – written in Alexandria, Virginia.

29. The End – written on September 4, 2014 in Alexandria, Virginia.

30. Spirit Guides – written on September 16, 2016 on flight UA4080, Lincoln, Nebraska to Chicago Illinois, Midwest USA.

Extras

Enjoy these unpublished works ...

One

Take a Moment and Reflect

Take a moment and reflect

on God's perfect love for you.

Take a moment and reflect

on my fallible love.

I fail you by my very existence,

still it must be enough for me.

It is all that I am, and steadier.

It walks towards the sea

in the perfect direction of the moon.

I am alone and I am not,

as I speak, as I think, as I breath.

It divides our highways, joins our world,

grows our substance in holy gardens

and listens for a Higher voice.

Blessed are you who follow your dreams.

Two

Royal Purple

Hewn royal purple

Such a deep feeling

Like a standing bass

Acoustic resonance expanding

Hollow wood and sinews drawn

Leather smells of earth

A slow leaning hand – managing metal

Building callouses against time

Fleur de lis – emblazoned and tasseled in gold

An ever-opening oak door.

Three

Never Knowing

Baby you will never know

What it means

to be in love with you

You're much too close

to who you've become

You'll never know

what it means to be lost in you

for you've found your way home

never knowing, sometimes disbelieving

And that's what is so enticing,

a hesitant innocence – non-conforming

Four

M Street

There is nothing on M Street

that can entice me

to live anymore – fully.

Masks and barricades of the hungry

shouting money from your pockets.

Society is divided – nothing new, or is there?

Rainbows dissected into color variants,

separated by familiar hues,

differences discarded into blackness,

corruption, greed, fear, hate, loss, pity, sympathy.

We fail and turn down into earthen vessels –

no choice but to participate.

Running left, running right,

hiding in plain sight.

Escaping no one, self-paralysis;

watching each tear as they pool.

Contributions from cultural angst run dry

and we mourn for each other,

despite our hate,

despite our ignorance,

despite our loss,

despite ourselves.

Five

Olive Leaves and Honey

The liquid sunshine had become too much a part of her, as if something unshakeable was looming. Forty days and forty nights, she thought, "why does this life have so many biblical parallels?" Her little house was like the Ark, with ants, bugs, and even raccoons, visiting in search of sanctuary. It seemed as though she had spent a lifetime plugging the holes to keep it afloat – this house, maybe life itself. There have been the challenges of rough water, but the horizon always seemed reachable – present.

The sounds that met her from the stereo across the room were penetrating and mysterious. Opus 72, Chopin's transcriptions for flute, floated and danced whimsically. She needed tea.

The kettle was large and silver with a spout that resembled an Arabian lamp's. Its use always invoked warm memories. It was a gift from a close friend in the Middle East, Abu Dula. She momentarily drifted to the desert, cross-legged and circle-seated, as the tea was poured and passed from hand to hand. The tea tasted better then, same kettle, same friends in the distance, but there was something about the moment that affected her from her soul to her taste buds. She missed those days – there was no concern of keeping her Ark afloat in a vast sea of sand. Orange Pekoe with a touch of honey; her usual break in time. "Not bad", she thought as the desert faded.

The sound of a Jay's call reached her, if not but for a moment – can it be? She curiously ventured to the door that led to the back of her world. The house had settled this past month. The rain eased the foundation's strength, entered the wooden supports and swelled them enough to make it difficult to free the door from its frame. She felt like a prisoner – tired. Three good nudges and the door creaked out and open. She envisioned a wave of water moving in to fill the space around her, expanding, never ending – filling her private places, her home, her soul.

A small drop of water fell at her feet as she looked skyward and saw the clouds parting ever so gently. The Jay called again, an invitation to proceed. Tea in hand, her bare feet eased across the wooden slats of the patio. She stood at the rail and searched for life. Then it came to her – she was the life for which she was searching.

ABOUT THE AUTHOR

John Edward Roessler (1962 -) was born in a small railroad town, Altoona, Pennsylvania, USA. He began reading and writing poetry in his teens. In 1984 he joined the U.S. Army and is now honorably retired. He has lived in various places throughout the United States and abroad. He holds a Master of Business Administration and is an educated Russian and Thai linguist and an avid reader of the classics. A motorcycle enthusiast, he enjoys traveling and creating food recipes for family and friends. He has four children, five grandchildren, and two Labradors. He lives with his wife, Watinee, in Alexandria, Virginia.

Your thoughts and words …

Your thoughts and words …

Your thoughts and words ...

Your thoughts and words ...